AF430676

PRAYERS FOR MORNING

TWENTY QUARTETS

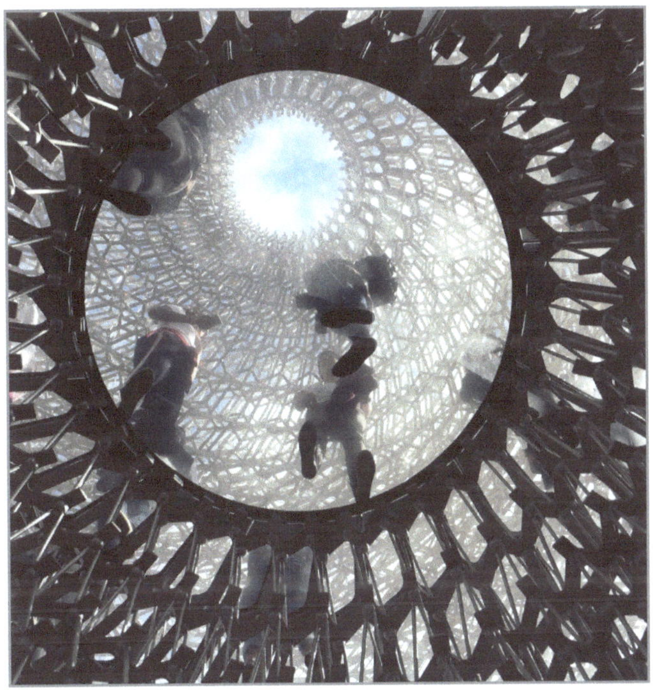

Prose poems by Kendall Johnson,
Kate Flannery, and John Brantingham

with artworks by Kendall Johnson

Prayers for Morning: Twenty Quartets

Visual art by Kendall Johnson, and prose poems by
Kendall Johnson, Kate Flannery, and John Brantingham

Copyrighted © 2024

ISBN: 979-8-3306-1238-3

Published by MacQ, Winston-Salem, North Carolina (USA)

Editing and book formatting are by Clare MacQueen. Book and cover design are by MacQueen in collaboration with Kendall Johnson.

Kendall Johnson: layeredmeaning@gmail.com

Kate Flannery: https://kateflannerywrites.com/contact

John Brantingham: https://www.johnbrantingham.com/contact-1

Clare MacQueen: macquinterly@gmail.com

Web addresses retrieved in November 2024.

For Clare MacQueen

Table of Contents

INTRODUCTION

This book is a collaboration among three writers, one of whom is also a visual artist. Each came to this project from a different perspective, a different concern for the world. Nevertheless, the common purpose that they share yields a unity of spirit. Four voices, three in word and one in image, creating a quartet.

Doom-scrolling media pulls me away from myself. While existential threats abound—climate breakdown, lethal division, political sociopathy, and war—addiction to media-induced hysteria is no answer. My prose poems and artworks, as two separate voices, make brief commentary on the runaway world of polarized politics, threats, fragmentation, and anonymity, portrayed by lead newscasts during Fall, 2023. Looking for balance from diverse spiritual traditions and from my own memories, I seek insight, direction. I seek hope.

—Kendall Johnson

Chaos, like Mount St. Helens, erupts with a roar. I look for foundations when chaos comes. I look to the sureness of the natural world, even when it is at its most destructive. The Pacific Northwest has been my foundation in those times. I am sustained by its rain, its steady gray, its vast, living expanse of coastlines that have seen repeated tsunamis, and I feel the strength of its wild mountains that have known eons of earthquakes. These things continue to reveal the calm and peace of Deep Time's continuum. This volume is reflective of those experiences, those times of prayer.

—Kate Flannery

I remember being a kid the day Mount St. Helens blew. That afternoon, I flew a kite in the California air and dreamed of ash blowing into it. I remember the first day of the Iraq War back in 1991. I was too old to fly a kite that day, but the wind was blowing. I stood outside in the cold evening and watched the trees in the schoolyard across the road shaking in the breeze. Always the wind has been a comfort. Always leaves move across the landscape. The wind will blow this evening. The wind will blow tomorrow no matter what we do.

—John Brantingham

Prayer I

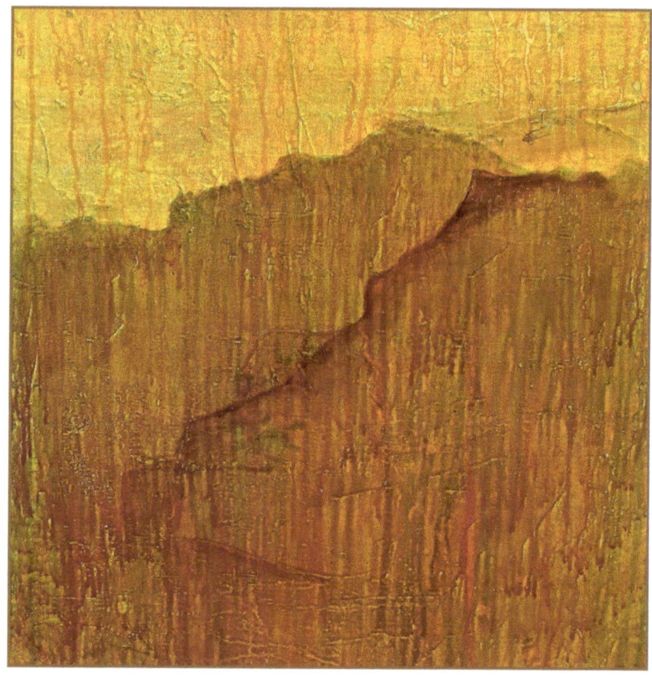

October 17, 2023

Family holds vigil for a Muslim mother hospitalized from a knife attack in Illinois. Her attacker was "upset" at events in the Middle East, where over a thousand Israelis were reported killed in a terror attack. In Yokosuka long ago, I watched drunken sailors and marines on night liberty, screaming, spitting, cursing at Japanese citizens walking by. Candles glowed softly in the night's darkness, in silent protest against the nuclear carrier just offshore.

Buddhists chant: *Hail to the jewel in the lotus.* It is said to calm fears, soothe concerns. Looking deeply within is said to even heal broken hearts. *Bring us compassion*, I pray.

White Gate

Beyond the white gate are the leaning stalks of Shasta Daisies, with their bitter green stems, lightly dusted with sticky floss, wanting to straggle away from my pruning shears; the plumed Phlox in colors of white, pink, and lavender, scented gently with a honeyed brightness; the clove-like spiciness of Stock, a rich flower almost made for eating. The taller elms and dogwood to the west shade them into growing toward the east, yet they are always reaching impossibly for the late afternoon sun.

Universal Corvid

The snow had melted off the city wall of Nanjing. I walked along the top, alone except for a guard. Crows circled above and called on a day too cold for walking or flying. The guard said something to me in Chinese, and I responded in English. He smiled and pointed at the birds.

They reminded me of the ravens in the Tower of London and crows in the High Sierra and all the magpies I had ever seen, even back to childhood. They spoke to us now in the universal language of birds, blessing or warning.

I couldn't tell.

Prayer II

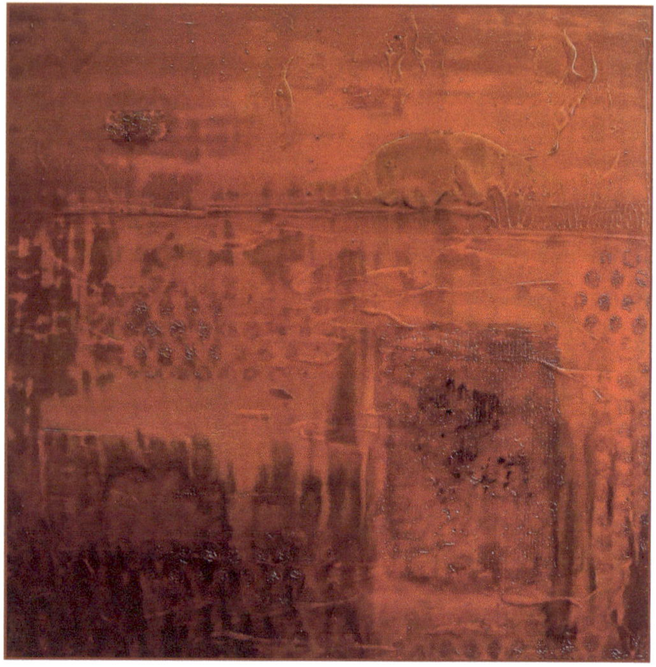

October 18, 2023

This morning's news reports how a bomb ripped through Gaza's largest hospital, killing 500 displaced civilians sheltering inside. Hamas was reported using hostages as shields. Children numbered heavily among the dead and injured. Protests have erupted across the world. Israel and Hamas trade blame. In this world of dazzle and propaganda, it is more comfortable to close our eyes and ears.

How to live in an insensitive world, yet keep my heart open for truth? Zoroastrians pray: *that understanding triumphs ... over indifference.* Help me to see beyond the propaganda. I pray I remain open to light.

River Rocks

My river rocks have tumbled down slabs of mountains, or sides of escarpments, first broken and cut by landslides. They begin with their sharp edges, until they become journey-weathered by water and sand and each other. Burnished until smooth. Hard and strong. Sleek with a soft coolness, their curves have symmetry and shine.

They ask to be held.

Forest Prayer

We were alone in camp when the satellite that had broken up in reentry lit up the forest. We counted 17 individual flaming pieces up there, each a different red, green, blue or yellow. We didn't know if it was a meteor or Elijah's chariot, so I asked, "Holy god, what is that?" sounding like a man in desperate need of an oracle, but there was no spiritualist here, only us, cut off from the city.

I remembered I had heard a rustling. Later, I would see the muddy print of a bear, who must have been watching over us.

Prayer III

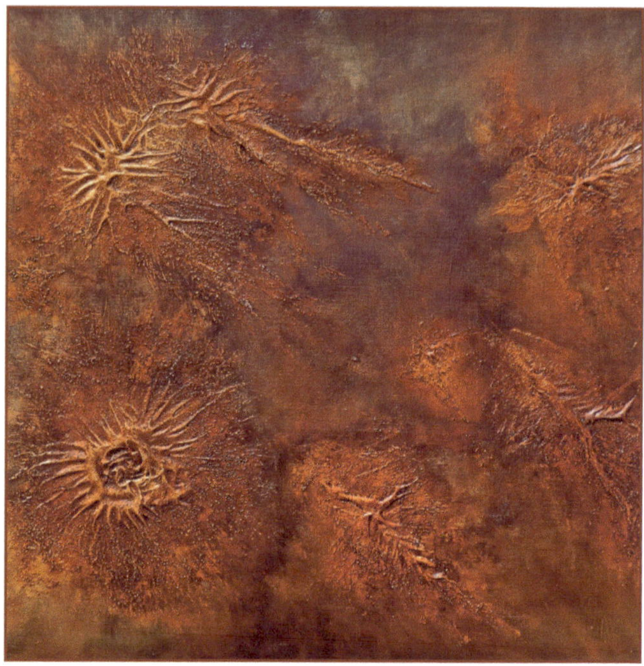

October 19, 2023

The Al-Ahli Hospital bombing occurred while Biden was visiting Israel. According to news reporters, Biden urged caution: "Don't be consumed by the rage," he said. "After 9/11, we were enraged, and we, too, sought justice. We also made mistakes." Indeed. Twenty years of over-reaction and war have left us divided, our Constitution in flames, whatever prestige we enjoyed in the world severely weakened.

The Sikhs point out: *Only that victory endures in consequence of which no one is defeated.* Help me to speak peace. Help me to be the prayer.

The Ancient One

He was designated "Kennewick Man" by the scientists who studied him, picking his 12,000-year-old bones apart. The scientists re-formed him after they had finished and turned him over to the local indigenous people for a quiet burial. Those people, whose tribal identities have been obliterated and re-formed over centuries, are now designated as the "Confederation of Tribes of the Colville Reservation." They were fierce in their fight to regain him—"The Ancient One"—because he was found in their region, and they have been there since the beginning of time.

September 12, 2001

The bear raised up when she heard me and the dog, and we stood, watching her there, not challenging, not worried, not anything but lost in that moment.

There was no outside of the bubble we had created near the crest of the mountain. Above us, the pine tops swayed wild, but here, in and among yellowing dogwoods there was a quiet.

The dog pressed himself against my leg. I wondered if there was a universe where the bear could do that, press herself against me for the comfort that connection brings. It wasn't this universe, but maybe it existed.

Prayer IV

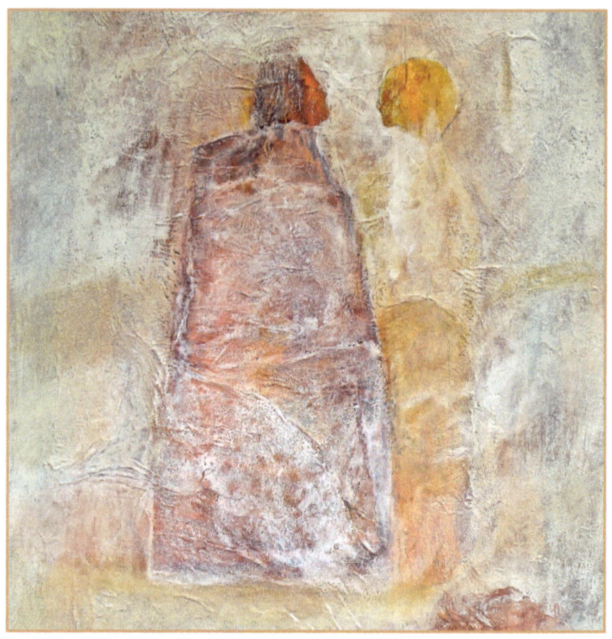

October 20, 2023

The House is considering a fear-driven defense-spending bill for next year topping 886 billion dollars. The bill guts abortion requirements, transgender medical care, and programs promoting diversity and inclusion.

Earlier this year, 62 diverse religious groups all signed a letter urging Congress to lower the proposed nearly one trillion dollars, arguing: *Some would be better spent on food, education, and medical care.*

I remind myself that we always breathe the shadow side of our all-too-fragile lives. It is within the face of the enemy, that we most clearly discern the shadow of our own.

Why Don't We Have More Lilacs?

I remember the lilacs of my childhood when we built fort frames with the lilacs' purple-filled branches and covered the frames with the sprawling vines of blue morning glories. We fought our child-battles with strategies for marauding and daring raids to capture neighbors' ripe plums. But by mid-afternoon the warm summer sun and the building lilac scent, like the scent of exotic lilies or mimosas, caused us to cease our fighting and doze in the grass while the wild bees joined us in our pausing. They say that lilacs can grow only in temperate climes, but their flowers can fight through old wood stems in order to bloom.

Down Below the Shale

This morning, I think about woodchucks hibernating down in the hole they've dug under my front step, way down beneath the layer of cracked shale, safe enough there to sleep for a season and a half. There are months for them to wander, and months for them to lie still.

This morning, I think of the dawn rising through the grove of giant sequoia trees, how I would have missed it if I'd stayed home. I think of the scent of orange blossoms at dusk in my childhood backyard, how I would have missed it if I wandered the earth.

PRAYER V

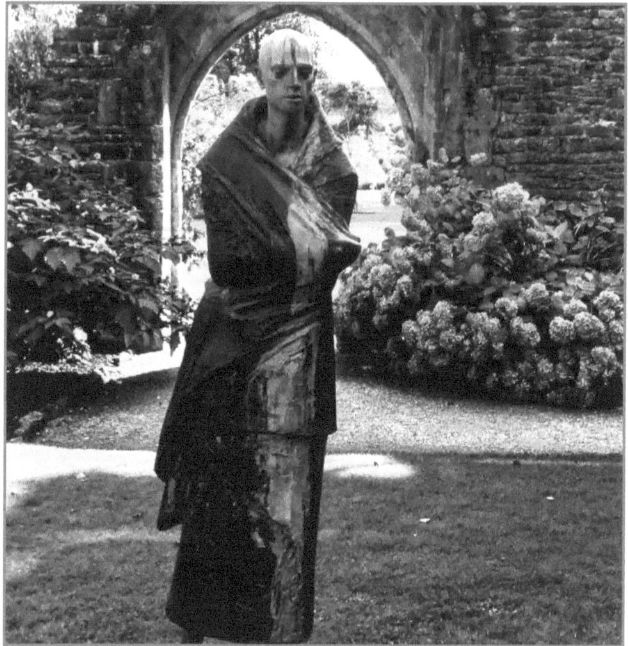

October 21, 2023

Fascist groups are again on the rise in the U.S. and abroad. Following ancient demagogic patterns, they blame minority ethnic groups as cause of discontent, fear of others they do not know, urge violence. When minds close to others, ears and fists follow. Incendiary words spawn repressive violence. Hate's cost is clear.

Spirits of the Sky and the Land, take the badness, disasters and sins, pray those of Shinto faith, *and purify all.*

Struggling to make sense of my fears, I must open my heart to others. I wrap myself in the promise of healing's path of light.

Pumice–1980

The mountain took its time. It heaved and shook for years before it shed 1100 feet of its summit, leaving downed forests, melted glaciers, and poisoned water in its wake. Some of the rocks and mud boiled into lehar and changed a small river from soft flow to roiling rage. The lehar took bridges, elk, trees, and the smallest of creatures. Other rocks began their long transformation, from untouchable fire into porous things so light and full of air when they cooled that they would float if I could toss them into the bluest water of the deep lake that is no longer there.

The Grove

That afternoon I wandered off trail to get to a grove of dogwood trees only I knew. It was white, blossoming spring, and the petals fell around me. I could hear the Peace Prayer of St. Francis, turned into a song, and I could hear the church sound women's voices chanting their rosaries. The grove was incensed with the white, blossom spring, and the wind coming off the Pacific carried the scent of salt spray. I thought of the dolphins of the ocean and the bears of the forest. I laughed as loud as I liked because I was alone.

Prayer VI

October 22, 2023

A solitary man sits, amidst Gaza rubble, where four stories have jumbled down upon his narrow street, with windows, doors, walls all blown into rubble. Hospitals, markets, mosques, churches, children, all targets. Pipes and wire hang empty, curtains all detritus. Toys, things of the living, now gone.

We have made you peoples and tribes, the Koran teaches us, *that you may know one another, not despise one another.* The man, alone, his life blasted away, speaks quietly into a phone. He waits for the tanks, as do we all. Help me to understand I am always that man.

Ghost Forest

I know a stand of grayed and withered remains of trees—hemlock and red cedars probably. Along the Copalis River on the Northern Coast—an old place of rich soil, soft clouds, and fern. The long-dead sentinels watch over what is left of the forest, killed by the coastal sea as a tsunami began its ride across the Pacific hundreds of years ago. As the ocean floor shuddered in a nearby fault, the wave began as a force with no hint of its coming power to kill by salt.

The Rubble

It's been over 100 years since the earthquake that destroyed San Francisco and raised the High Sierra nearly twenty feet, and the rocks and boulders, some the size of houses, that churned from the earth still lie around you in the meadows and saddles. Small creatures live underneath them and in their crevasses.

Sometimes on your morning hike, you'll realize a whole colony of marmots watch you from the safety of that rubble. Their tunnels radiate below, so they can disappear if you act on the predator nature baked into your DNA if you are not content simply to watch.

Prayer VII

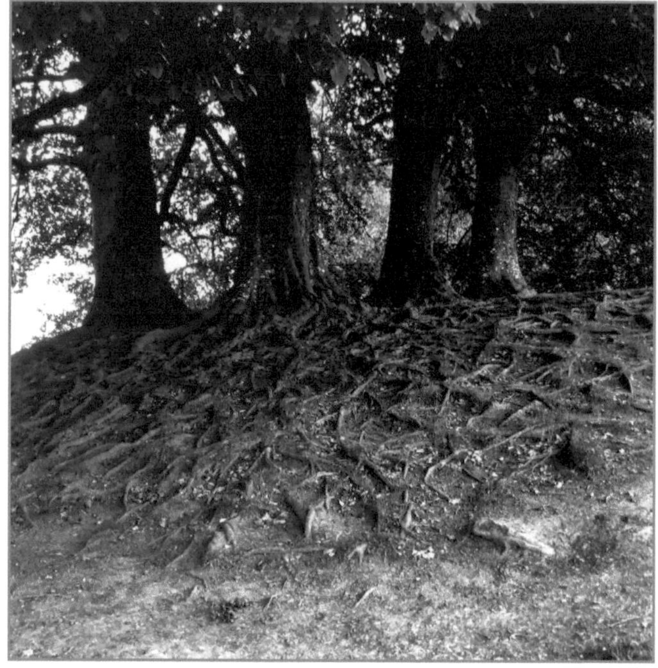

October 23, 2023

Dark Gaza tunnels await us all: a labyrinthine trap baited with bunkers. Explosive devices await, a thousand Minotaurs hidden in darkness. I remember how tunnels won the Vietnam war, re-supply freeways moving troops, minds, hearts. Flashlights and pistols proved more powerful than those five million tons of bombs. Tunnels of darkness, vital light lost.

The Jains pray: *Do not injure any living being ... the eternal way of spiritual life.* Injustice creates rage, which in turn grows blind. I pray I can remember to see from both sides.

And from above as well. I can speak out, but must open my heart.

Beach Pines

The oldest pines I have seen in the wild places of the Oregon coast have graceful, twisted trunks, partly because of the coastal winds' shaping, and partly because of the trees' habit, a tendency to reach outward rather than upward. My visits to local nurseries present arrays of specimen pines, displayed in their clean boxes for the wealthy from Portland who come on weekends to enjoy their leisure and their garden parties. Those trees, needing richer soil, do not fare well in the sand of the North Coast. But the seedlings of the older trees I find on my coastal walks grow fast and give me squirrels for company and shade when the sun blazes.

Bristlecones and Bats

We drove into the White Mountains among bristlecone pines, five thousand years old or so, just waiting as they've waited for a while now.

We hadn't learned about these trees. To us they were gnarled perches for turkey vultures if we noticed them at all on our way to the mine shafts we wanted to explore, now that miners had abandoned them to the desert.

Inside the mines, colonies of bats hung upside down until dusk when they would fly out, swirling around us and the trees, us ancient compared to the bats and a mere glimmer compared to the trees.

Prayer VIII

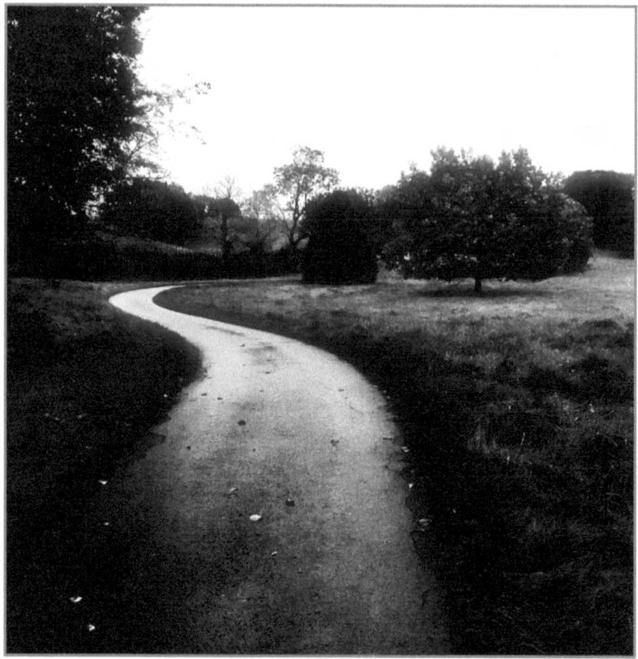

October 24, 2023

Silence sweeps the world this morning, in response to the murderous death grip in the Ukraine. Threats escalate and neighbors look for advantage. Years ago Walt Disney illustrated the effects of atomic fission by tossing a ping pong ball into an empty room filled with set mousetraps covering the floor. On each, two ping pong balls rested motionless. One lone ball arcs toward the floor. The entire room turns into chaos.

A Shinto prayer: *I pray that the wind will soon puff away the clouds hanging over tops of mountains.* I must remember that it matters what I myself do.

Kites in the Wind

Running with kites flying behind offers a singular pleasure to children and dogs. Kites, like flags waving high, are pulled along by high energy and unrelenting purpose. The children find their freedom's pride as they push against the headwinds. They do not see or feel the coming storm.

Crossing the Ridge

The trail is in charge of everything in your life at this moment. Let your mind wander into the waking dream the rhythm of your steps makes when it mixes with the scents of the river, trees, and bears all around you.

Your feet take you across the ridge, and the forest stretches out before you, all the way to Lake Erie. As you wander through, the birds sing about you, all of them telling each other that you have entered the woods.

If you listen closely enough, you can hear them saying that it matters that you are here.

Prayer IX

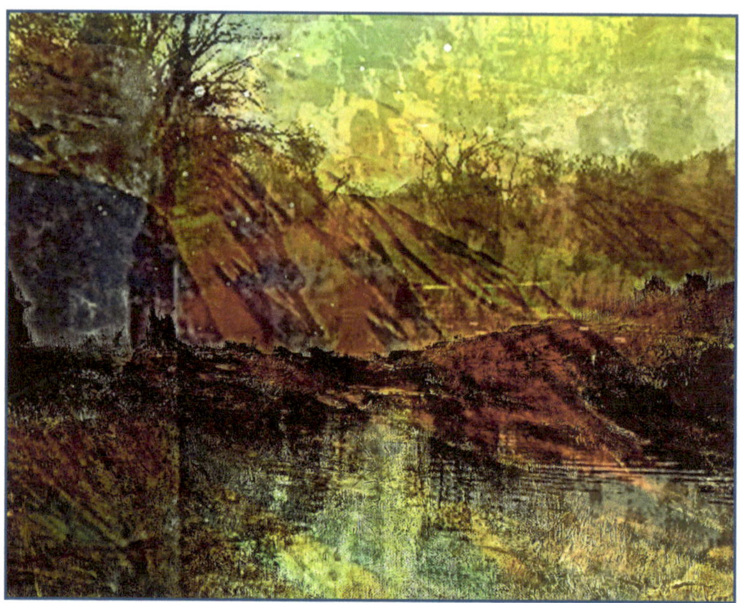

October 25, 2023

Hamas operatives kill over a thousand Israelis in a devastating terror attack on October 7. The ensuing retaliation is overwhelming. When the United Nations chief suggests that Hamas did not act in a vacuum, that the attack was spawned by decades of oppression, the Israeli Prime Minister labels him a terrorist and calls for his head. We sometimes become that which we most hate.

The Buddhists pray: *May those frightened cease being afraid, and may those bound be free.* May I find the courage to voice opposition to injustice, and at the same time assuage fear. May I find holy light in the balance.

New Growth

Over 60 people died when Mount St. Helens exploded in May of 1980.   Some stubbornly refused to evacuate in spite of the warnings, some came to watch and report, some were simply there because they always came to the mountain's surrounding forests in May—to camp, to walk, to sleep and find peace among the trees.

And a year after the blast, my mother's camellias burst into the longest spring growth, caused by the acid ash that had rained down on her garden after the mountain changed everything.

Moments in Between

The police must have come through announcing the fire was coming, and that we needed to evacuate the mountain, but we slept through their warnings, waking to a forest of birdsong, the cars gone, gone the sounds of neighbor fighting, gone the sound of tourists flying drones so they could see the trees they stood next to, but from above. The freight-train roar of fire was coming and falling trees and exploding trunks and the sound of people's houses wiped from the earth, but now, between when we woke and when we fled, it had gone back to being forest.

Prayer X

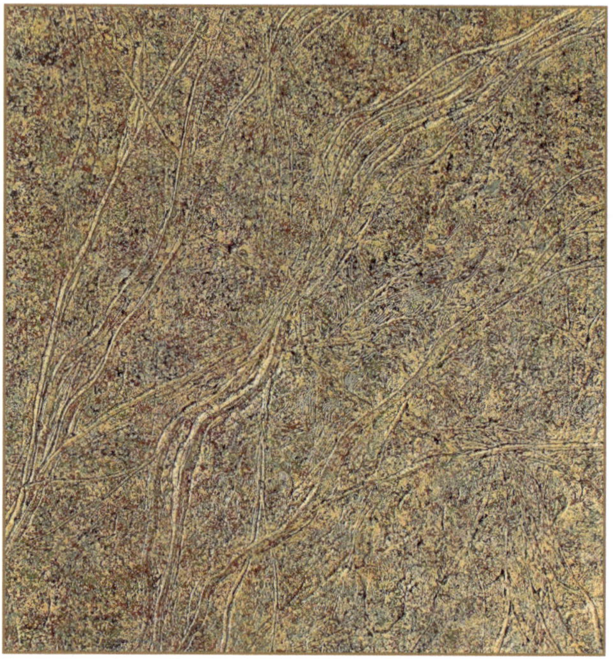

October 26, 2023

The 92nd Street Y in uptown New York has cancelled the next speaker in its writer's center program, who has been censored for speaking out against war. The resulting writers' backlash caused the entire program to fold. The 92NY Center thus fails its own stated mission and purpose, to help people find their voice.

A Buddhist prayer: *May those who find themselves in trackless, fearful wildernesses be guarded.* Peaceful dissent is freedom's necessary voice. Help me be open to what others say, and help me speak with courage and compassion. This will define who we all will become.

Shifting Dunes

The beaches in Oregon grow and reduce as the storms attack the sand from the west and from the south. Every winter the tumult remakes the landscape. Salt and wind conspire and combine to chew at the edges of the coast, creating new dunes, new forms. But the creatures who live there persist. Elk, sandpipers, loons, beach pea and wild strawberry shift their ground easily. But the people have the hardest time of it. Because at other edges of the water, the storms give back what they've taken elsewhere, and houses that once had ocean views now see only high bleak dunes, strands of kelp, and broken shells forming litter beyond.

Even Before Ur

I was in among the trees off trail, cutting across the woods with my dog when the coyotes started their yammering around us, not the howling of television cartoons, but clipped yips, maybe 10 of them all at once saying something to each other untranslatable to human speech but clear enough to me and the dog.

It was like a prayer for persistence, a call from a pre-Ur language that rumbled under our skins from a group of animals that had been hated and cast out and hunted but survived for as long as humans had the words for hatred.

Prayer XI

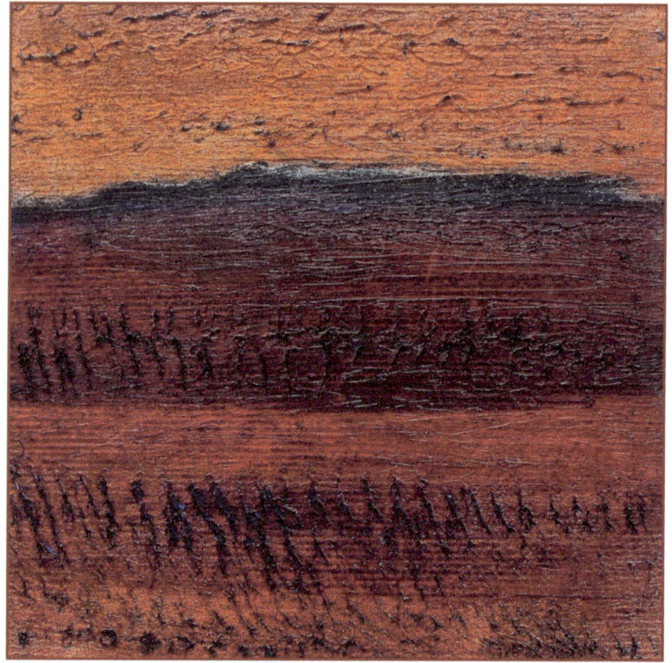

October 27, 2023

Israel sends a tweet to Gaza: "For your safety, escape to the south."
1. The message is in English (which *neither* side speaks);
2. Gaza had been blacked-out (*no one* could get the text);
3. Black-out hinders relief and rescue, but not bombs.

Tanks move into Gaza, and a protective border disappears. Hamas exposes the tweet to the press. Propaganda mills churn on through the night: the world's heart strings are played like a Stradivarius.

A Zoroastrian prayer: *Let trust triumph over contempt, and truth triumph over falsehood.* Help me to see past my limitations, to see light beyond the thicket.

Fort Stevens

They built the fort at the Columbia's mouth for a world at war. Its ten-inch guns with a nine-mile range were never fired against a foe, despite the years of practice. Command now gone, the old men acting as tour guides note the vacant shell rooms and the rusted hoists. They speak with pride of guns that shook the ground. While an empty gun-pit sends up soft grass thrusting through the rock and a thriving ragwort weed that's shuddering in the wind.

That Evening

On 9/11 I was in the forest and didn't know about the towers until the world found its newest reason for rage. I remember the evening skies being clear. Maybe they were. I remember Venus through the trees and seeing Mars clearly red. Who knows? Maybe I did.

I remember the wind through the trees brought in the vanilla scent of Jeffrey pines warmed by the late summer air and the way I could hear coyotes calling to each other with the same conversation coyotes have been having since they began to talk.

I remember understanding what they said.

Prayer XII

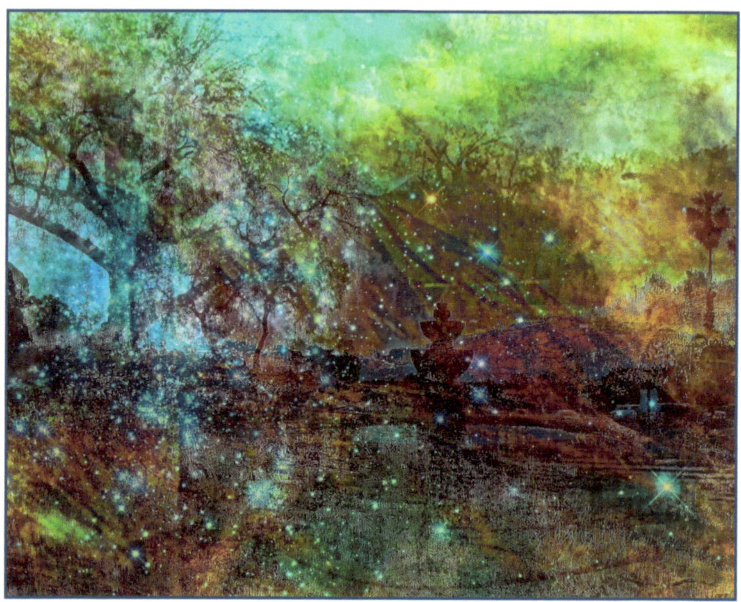

November 5, 2023

I awaken to news that the Koreas have each suspended their own ban on spy satellites, because they heard the other did the same. Threats and counter threats, fighting and retaliation. Chronic anger roils at enforced anonymity, corporate conditioning, and our uncontrolled digitized lives. My dreams reflect despair, my growing sense of precious waters circling the drain.

Oh God, lead us from the unreal to the Real, the Hindus pray. If I can break the media-induced trance, fears reduce to reality-size, and I can slow my approach down to only the speed of life. Grant me the courage to turn down the volume.

Slash Burning

The burning of slash is an old way of living. Men leaving behind the slash and shreds of their work to be burned on the land. The fire will smolder on for days, showing no flames, no blaze of heat that you can see. The burn continues for the longest time; it never seems completely out. Just under the surface, leaving an ash and hope that all this brings a better soil. But soon it wastes away, and there comes the fallow field, a barren land after all that work. Until a new season.

Liquid Caves

Sometimes I dream of the waters of my childhood mountains. In the High Sierra, water leeches slowly through caves and what goes in might not come out for a hundred years. The rain that fell on me when I was a child, might be flowing into a stream where another kid swims today.

When I dream of those waters, everything seems more real than my waking world, or it feels more right. I am in my proper place, and this earth is in a balance. I do not dream of chronic anger or threats. Leave that to the waking world.

Prayer XIII

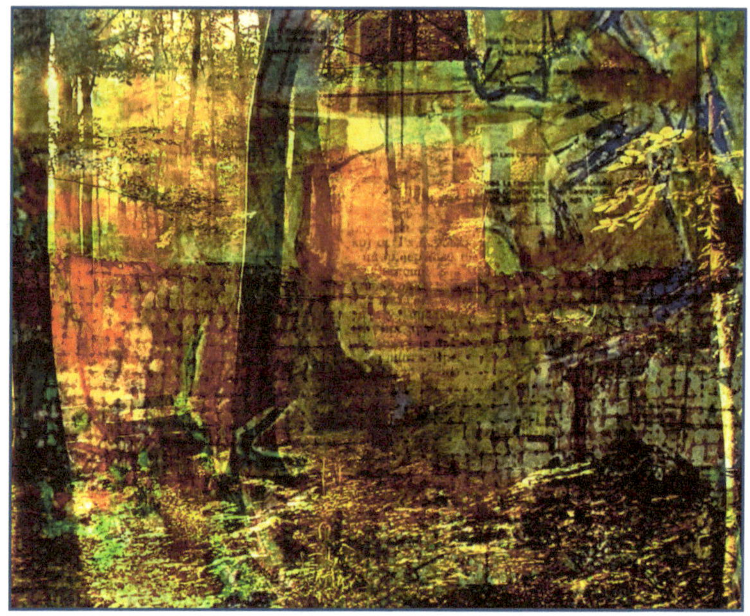

November 13, 2023

Since Covid, global flash points have re-ignited with vengeance: regional wars, tipping-point climate destruction, political fracture. Beyond *Future Shock*, 2023 has birthed a crisis in the meaning of truth and belief. Challenges to epistemic foundations undermine trust. Uncertainty becomes the new terror, anger the new god.

The Koran reminds us: *Grant us a healthy heart and a truthful tongue.* As a member of my family, my community, I must persevere. I must not fall for the easy answers of blaming and violence. For those whom I love, I must stay awake. For the sake of the light, I cannot yet sleep.

Nurse Log

In the woods of the Pacific Northwest, change often happens from "disturbances," the forces of forest succession and forest tolerance —with competing and cooperating trees. And fires, wind, floods, avalanches, disease, volcanoes, and people all play their part. An old tree falls slowly with the sound of cracking and breaking. The grouse, nuthatches, and warblers who knew the tree hear the fall. Saplings, seedlings, and understory feel the fall. And by some grace, a few of the tree's roots still hold fast to the soil, yielding up moisture and nutrients and quiet haven.

The Memory of the Nurse Remained

Two thousand years into its life, I hiked by the sequoia tree for the first time. By then, it had wrapped its roots around a boulder and hung there in the air, probably offspring of a nurse tree that had died there hundreds of years before it sprouted. The weight of all of that lingered at the edge of the meadow.

I thought that in the time it had been sitting there, ancient gods had disappeared and with them nations that birthed them and the reasons their citizens hated outsiders.

In that time, even the mountains had risen a bit.

Prayer XIV

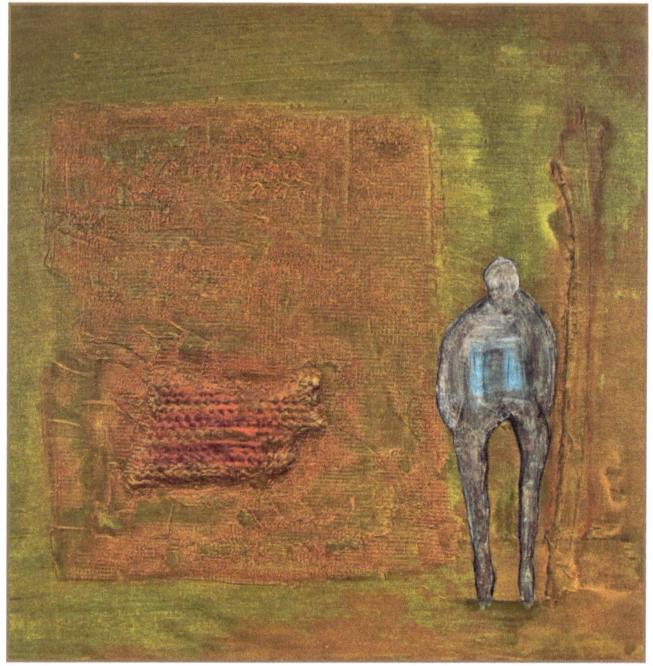

November 14, 2023

Médecins Sans Frontières doctors report troops sniping civilians attempting to flee the Al-Shifa hospital, whom they had ordered to leave. The doctors are bound by medical ethics; patients are without food, power, nursing, or supplies. Snipers fear the lethal loss of leverage if enemies are allowed to escape. A perverse and deadly Catch-22.

A Hebrew prayer: *God is filled with loving sympathy for human frailty*. Rage and fear strip away our humanity. Help me learn to determine just action, using my imagination and compassion. Help me recall a better version of who we all are, what we might someday come to be.

Sand Dollar

You'll never find these creatures with their soft, velvety covering of filigreed fringe, when they are deep in the sea and settled into the sand below. They are not like the spiny urchins, purple and bright red, that are pulled from the sea and split apart for the culinary delight of those with refined tastes. When you find a sand dollar on the beaches of the North Coast, only their outer protective shell remains, with the soft petal-like remnant of the creature's shape etched on top. A delicate flower pattern where the creature breathed. The urchin has left its art behind, now bleached by the sun and battered by the waves.

This Fragility

On the trail, I take a bad step and twist my ankle and curse and shout and limp around in a circle, trying to work out the ache, trying to ignore the frailty inherent in my body, my softness, my fragility. This vulnerability is what will kill me, stop my heart or eat me from within.

I tell myself that this soft body isn't me. It's just the thing that carries me through this world of cities, forests, and beaches. It's there to fail me, to show me how to find strength inside when there is so little on the outside.

Prayer XV

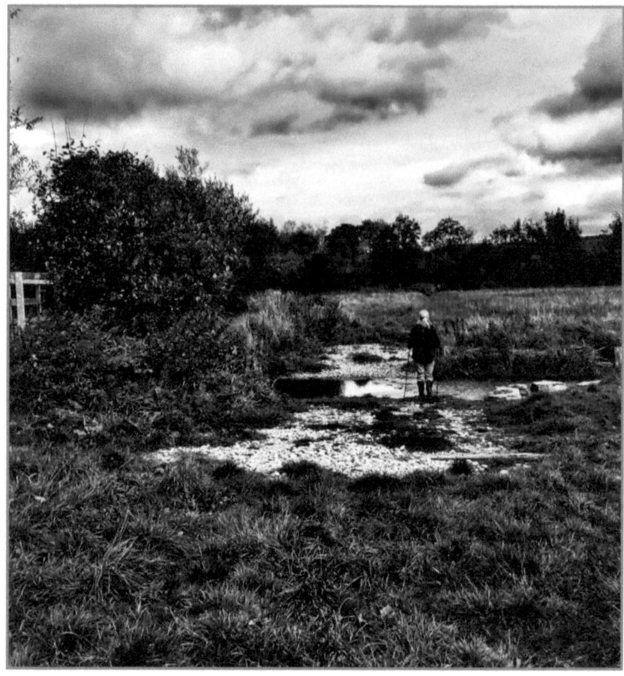

November 21, 2023

This morning France test-fired its long-range ballistic missile, in the face of Putin's repeated nuclear saber-rattling. He doesn't want NATO sending arms to Kiev. Rattled, India puts Pakistan on notice. China and North Korea trade threats.

There is nothing that affects one of us, the Jesuits pray, *that does not affect us all*. I look to my grandchildren's future, and I don't know what to say. Fearful of oncoming trains, I am tempted to distrust all approaching lights and freeze. Yet if I am to reach the end of this tunnel, I must open to the light.

Old Barn I

Lack of purpose on the barn's part, and apathy on the owner's part are reasons why a Northwest barn decays and molders. And once the process starts, the moss begins its slow creep onto the carcass of the barn. Vines and brambles climb its sides and ride its roof until the thing caves at the center and begins a slow bend toward the ground. Children do not play there, farm animals do not shelter there, and old men do not drink alone there any more.

The Music of Robins

As I stand still on the trail to look over the marsh, I hear the robins' music change because I'm not crashing through. It changes again when an old couple walks by. I know they're in the forest before I see them. Which is just to say that what one creature does in the forest affects us all, or at least, we notice if we're quiet and focused on this moment. It's winter now, so the deer that walk through these trees are the ones who made it through the hunting season. It seems to me they are calmer now.

Prayer XVI

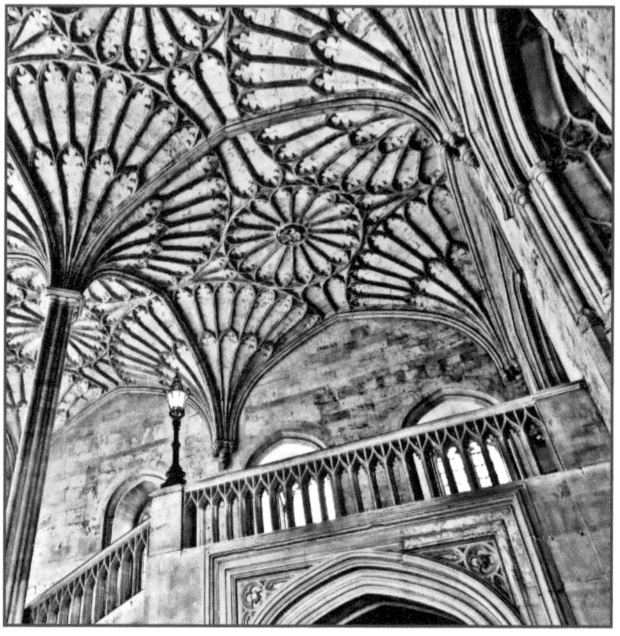

November 22, 2023

Beset by legal consequences after his illegal acts, a politician resorts to even more incendiary rhetoric. "Death to my opponents," he cries, "vermin!" Wishing to expand federal powers and eliminate those against him, he praises Mussolini, Stalin, Putin. Such speeches will goad mindless followers to violence, disrupting peaceful process, he hopes, eclipsing his 91 pending felony charges. His supporters are undeterred.

Concluding a conference, Pope John Paul II prayed: *Let us go; let us weave the tapestry of peace with the golden threads of justice, freedom, and forgiveness.* Which call I choose to follow, hope or hate, is my own call to make.

Old Barn II

There is no calculation that can justify a barn's upkeep in the face of its steady dying, the slow weakening, the thinning of its bones, its muscles turning slack and full of wither. The old man who used to tend the fields nearby and used to store the new grain in the younger barn now ends each day clasping his bottle of rye while sitting on a rotting bale.

And no one passes by and watches as it happens.

The Music of Woodpeckers

My mother's religious fervor might be what I respected most about her, how she'd take her rosary with her on vacation, almost always to the forest. I watched her once standing at the base of a giant sequoia praying, fingering her beads. I remember the call of a pileated woodpecker, that loud eerie cry, and then it was there above her, and she didn't see or hear it because she was praying for the peace Pope John Paul II told her could come as a result of prayer. Peace has not come yet, but still she prays for it daily.

Prayer XVII

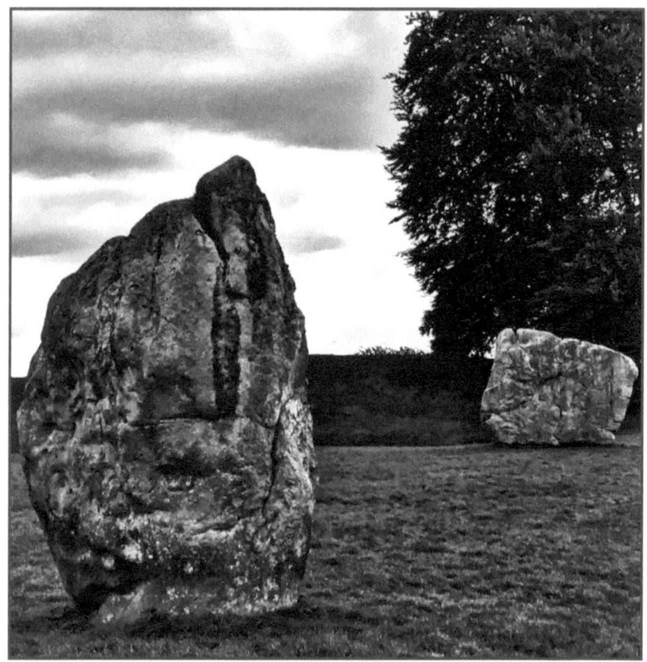

November 27, 2023

The nuclear arms race is on again. More countries have bigger devices, non-state entities have smaller. Threats are tossed around as if nuclear strikes could be a new, sustainable norm. More players with more weapons now, more volatility and less reason. The age-old strategy of inadequacy: impressing others with one's size.

Recovery programs pray: *God grant me the serenity to accept the things I cannot change, the courage to change those things I can, and the wisdom to know the difference.* Help me, help all of us, to discern the underlying hunger, to find ways to meet that need.

Sleeping with the Surf

It is not a comfort on the North Coast as some might think. It does not lull the mind to sleep and dream so near the Columbia. There, Pacific tides persist with an unrelenting eastern push. The river too must have its way and will not compromise its westward surge. I cannot rest while ocean surf creates its loud and crashing pulse, an unrelenting drive for something solid, something larger, something sure. Something else.

The Day After That

When they'd make me watch Cold War movies like *The Day After* or *Red Dawn*, I'd retreat into a fantasy where I could disappear into the woods if it came to that, a sylvan life by myself and away from hatred. It was naive, but no more so than the plots of those movies. Then we'd retreat into the mountains for a week in summer. On solo hikes, I'd daydream that the cities were gone. Soon it didn't matter whether they were or not. All that mattered was this moment, and then the next, each moment sacred like a prayer.

Prayer XVIII

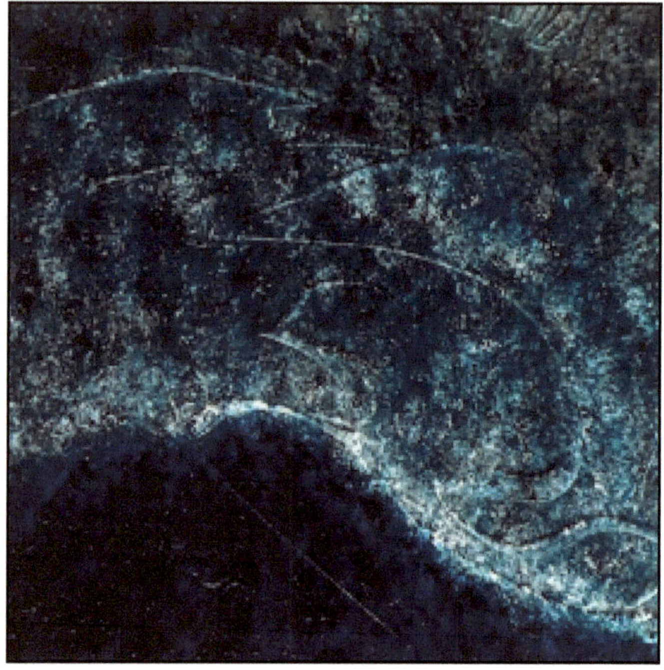

November 28, 2023

Three Arizona university students are shot, walking to a relative's home for Thanksgiving. Two were American citizens, one a legal resident. Two were wearing Keffiyeh scarves at the time, bold fishnet and olive-leaf black and white designs, signifying strength, resilience, and perseverance. A community fractured.

When old lodestars no longer map our territory, it is time to look for more solid ground. Navajo pray that they may: *walk in beauty … be a bond between the Worlds of Earth and Spirit.* Their traditional hogan doors face east, always open to the promise of rising sun. I too try to open to interior lighting.

Ragwort

Jacobaea vulgaris

They go where they're not wanted. Somewhat weedy, they straggle on beaches trying to establish themselves. Their seeds are carried by winds and birds until the grains find some friendly soil. Local farmers, whose business it is to produce and sell, have wrongly blamed the plant and charge that ragwort kills their herds and flocks. But if it is allowed to live, it feeds the brightly colored moths named Meadow Brown, Gatekeeper, and Holly Blue.

Every Morning

My first solo backpacking trip, I rose with the dawn. I'd awakened in the dark hours, when I heard black bears pawing around my camp, and the full moon had brought me out of the tent earlier than that when I'd thought it was the first light of morning. Here it was at last blazing the eastern sky.

You can use words like "sacred," but a moment like that is sacred only inside silence, and at 15 I wouldn't have known to use that word anyway, but I was alone with the bear, ravens, and crow and it sanctified my morning.

Prayer XIX

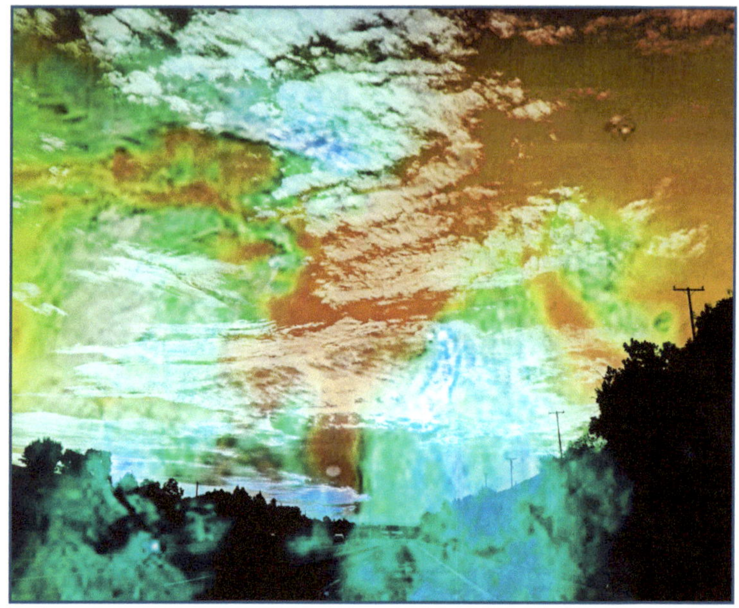

November 29, 2023

Controversy. Documents just surfaced indicate that the president of COP28, this year's UN conference for climate change being held in Dubai, has set agenda talking-points for meetings with 15 other governments to expand the UAE's oil interests (United Arab Emirates). "Breathtaking hypocrisy," newspapers cry, and a "moment of truth for the oil industry." A truth once simply "inconvenient" now laps squarely upon our shores.

Greed and deceit are only part of human nature. A Sufi prays: *Dispel the mists of illusion from the hearts of the nations.* The question is, how long will change take over there, and in my heart here at home?

Thlakalamah

The Kalama begins its journey on the remaining flank of Mount St. Helens. Remember the river's glacial water and wandering ways—sometimes slow, sometimes swift. Shaped and eroded by lahars and rock hurling out from the volcano eons ago. The tread of its trails is primal pumice. The river offers steelhead in icy green water and a cold that will stop your breath.

Season of Mist

Two days of rain has melted the snow, and now we're in a season of mists, a kind of liminal time that's neither winter nor spring. I can't see far this week because of it, but that just means I drive slowly or not at all. I take time to pick up a stone and turn it over in my hand and understand it in that way that goes beyond words. Soon, the insects will wake up and reptiles will thaw out, and the world will be noisy. For now, I feel like the only one awake in the house.

Prayer XX

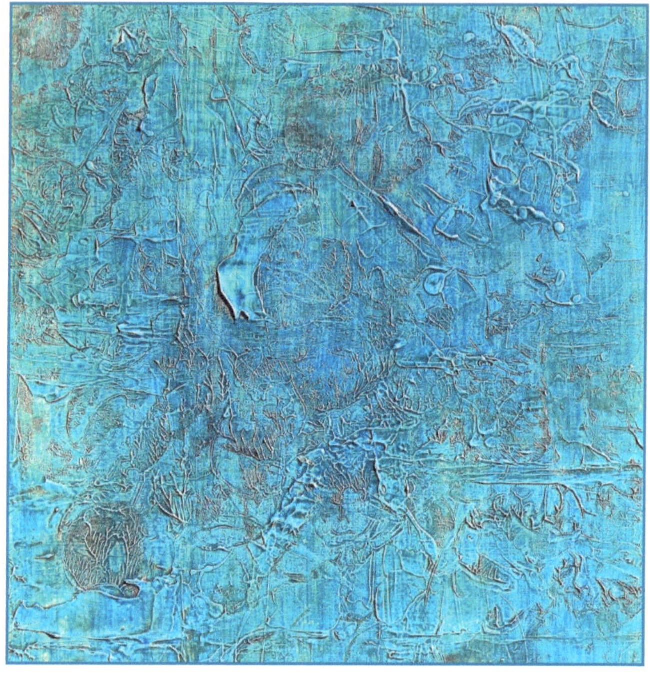

December 31, 2023

This morning I read that the U.S. is "capitalizing" the policy of "mutually assured destruction" (MAD) to the tune of 1.5 trillion dollars. The plan calls for reduction in conventional arms spending even though risk of conventional war is escalating.

Those following the Baha'i faith pray: *Whatever decreaseth fear increaseth courage.* Imagination can both intimidate and empower, and the art of creative construction remains a formidable wild card. I remind myself that moving into creative action channels fear. I can write letters and books, paint signs. I can chant. It is time again to resist. Time to move upward toward light.

Orca

whose name means "of the kingdom of the dead"

We hear them before we see them. Their breathing pushes the air in churns and rushes like a trumpet's blast calling each other to war. A sound heard for miles. Slipping through the Kitsap waters in the south of the Salish Sea, they hunt safely in their pods, herding salmon into shallow bays where there is no escape. Grown fat and friendly, the orcas never venture into larger waters. Everything they need is within their reach.

Morning of the Bear

I was just a kid when I learned that California black bears weren't out to get me and didn't have anything of a passing interest in me. Once on a trail in pine shade along a steep hill, I came around a corner to find a male walking my way. We both stopped and considered each other in the sharp morning cool, looking into each other's eyes for a moment that was eternal and over almost immediately. Then he stepped off the path just as I backed up as if we were both trying to decrease the other's fears simultaneously.

End Notes

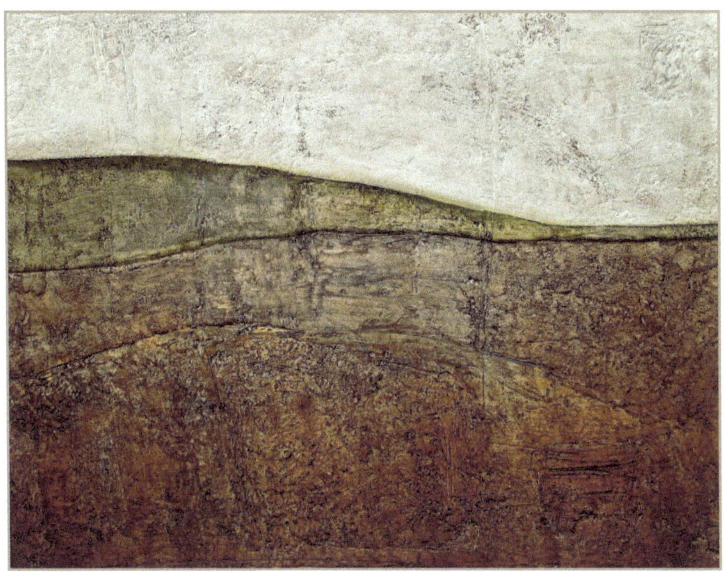

Postlude

Originally, I set out to lend voice to those oppressed by the swarm of toxic world events that seemed to me overwhelming in the Fall of 2023: climate breakdown, political fracture, and the saturation of media trance. The emerging tragedy of Gaza seemed to epitomize the moment: a collapse of human reason, and some might say civilization. I soon realized that my collection of scribblings during this time needed to bring more to readers: an alternative way of viewing the world.

I brought poetic pieces to our writing group. Based on their comments I asked John Brantingham and Kate Flannery to join me by giving alternative ways of seeing things. Their work added depth and purpose, and we named the resulting pieces "quartets."

In my discussions with publisher Clare MacQueen, I mentioned this project and process, and she was intrigued. I sent her a piece (one of the quartets with three pieces plus my artwork) and she asked to publish it. She fit our work into an already busy publishing schedule. Beyond getting a publisher, we gained a partner, a true collaborator who shared our goal of adding something of value to a hurting world.

Speaking for all of us, we are immeasurably grateful for Clare's wise counsel along with her warm and enthusiastic support for our work. Hers is the quiet fifth voice in our prayerful quartets.

—Kendall Johnson
November, 2024

Art Credits

Prayers in Image by Kendall Johnson

Collaborator Bios

Kendall Johnson grew up in the lemon groves in Southern California, raised by assorted coyotes and bobcats. A former firefighter with military experience, he served as therapist and crisis consultant—often in the field. As psychologist and trauma specialist, he has written several non-fiction books and numerous articles on trauma and school crisis. He trained crisis teams and rendered direct support following numerous natural disasters, school shootings, and 9/11.

As a nationally certified teacher, he taught art and writing, served as a gallery director, and still serves on the board of the Sasse Museum of Art, for which he authored the museum books *Fragments: An Archeology of Memory* (2017), an attempt to use art and writing to retrieve lost memories of combat, and *Dear Vincent: A Psychologist Turned Artist Writes Back to Van Gogh* (2020). He holds national board certification as an art teacher for adolescents to young adults.

Kendall retired from teaching and clinical work a few years ago to pursue painting, photography, and writing full time. In that capacity he has written five literary books of artwork and poetry; one art-history book; and a hybrid collection of essays, memoir, poetry, and visual art, *Writing to Heal: Self-Care for Creators* (MacQ, May 2024).

He's the author of *The Stardust Mirage* (Cholla Needles Press, 2022), *Black Box Poetics* (Bamboo Dart Press, 2021), and *Chaos & Ash*, a memoir collection (Pelekinesis, 2020). His Fireflies series is published by Arroyo Seco Press: *Fireflies Against Darkness* (2021), *More Fireflies* (2022), and *The Fireflies Around Us* (2023).

Shorter work has appeared in *Chiron Review, Cultural Weekly, Literary Hub, MacQueen's Quinterly, Quarks Ediciones Digitales,* and

Shark Reef, and was translated into Chinese by *Poetry Hall: A Chinese and English Bi-Lingual Journal.*

Kendall is a contributing editor for *The Journal of Radical Wonder*: https://medium.com/@kendalljohnson_94480

His website: http://www.layeredmeaning.com

Kate Flannery is an Editor-at-Large for *The Journal of Radical Wonder*, where she writes the bi-weekly column "Interludes." She is also a writer, lawyer, and musician who lives in a small college town. Her essays, poetry, and fiction have been published in *Chiron Review*, *The Ekphrastic Review*, *Emerge*, *MacQueen's Quinterly*, *Pure Slush*, and *Shark Reef*. In 2022, she was a finalist for *Bellingham Review*'s Annie Dillard Award for Creative Nonfiction.

She works regularly with the Sasse Museum in Pomona, California, contributing to exhibition catalogs for the museum as well as writing ekphrastic poetry in response to the artwork on display there. Her current projects are a curated volume about Palmer Canyon in the wake of the Grand Prix Fire of 2003 and a collection of reflections on the 2024 death of her brother: *A Book of Michael —Presence, Absence, and Things In Between.*

Kate's website: https://kateflannerywrites.com/about

John Brantingham's work has been made possible by a grant from the New York State Council on the Arts. He was the first poet laureate of Sequoia and Kings Canyon National Parks (east of Fresno, California), and now lives in Jamestown, New York.

The founder and general editor of *The Journal of Radical Wonder*, he is also the author of 21 books of poetry, memoir, and fiction, including his latest, *Days of Recent Divorce* (Arroyo Seco Press, 2023); *Life: Orange to Pear* (Bamboo Dart Press, 2020); and *Kitkitdizzi* (Bamboo Dart Press, 2022), the latter a collaboration which features artworks by his wife, Ann Brantingham.

John's poems, stories, and essays are published in hundreds of magazines and journals. His work has appeared on Garrison Keillor's daily show, *The Writer's Almanac*; has been nominated multiple times for the Pushcart Prize; and was selected for publication in the *Best Small Fictions* anthology series for 2022 and 2016.

He co-edited *The L.A. Fiction Anthology* (Red Hen Books), and is a fiction editor for *Chiron Review.* He currently teaches online through the Inlandia Institute and in person at Chautauqua Gallery in Jamestown, New York.

John's website: https://www.johnbrantingham.com/

Clare MacQueen is founding editor and curator of the online arts and literary journal *MacQueen's Quinterly*, aka MacQ, launched on New Year's Day, 2020, and its precursor *KYSO Flash* (2014–2019). She edited, designed, and produced 20 printed books, including six annual anthologies, via KYSO Flash Press (retired March 2020).

Via MacQ, she has published five books, including a collection of flash literature by Daryl Scroggins, *The Light I Want to Keep* (December 2024); and four collaborations with others: *Triggered: A Pillow Book* (Autumn 2023) with poet Alexis Rhone Fancher and visual artist Kenna Barradell; *Writing to Heal: Self-Care for Creators* (Spring 2024) with poet/visual artist Kendall Johnson; *Because the World Is Spinning* (Autumn 2024) with poet/dancer Marcus Elman; and *Prayers for Morning: Twenty Quartets*, with poets Kendall Johnson, Kate Flannery, and John Brantingham (December 2024). Forthcoming early in 2025: *Crazy Bitches: selected haibun*, a collaboration with poet Roberta Beary.

With Lorette C. Luzajic, Clare co-edited *The Memory Palace: An Ekphrastic Anthology* (March 2024). As webmaster and an associate editor for *Serving House Journal* (2010-2018), Clare helped publish 18 online issues. And she's one of four co-editors of *Steve Kowit: This Unspeakably Marvelous Life* (Serving House Books, 2015).

She was also honored to serve as one of two judges for the 2017 Steve Kowit Poetry Prize and as one of three finalist judges for the Jack Grapes Poetry Prize in 2021. For several years, she's served on the Senior General Advisory Board for *Best Small Fictions*.

After living and working 16 years in San Diego and 25 years in the northern Puget Sound area, Clare left the West Coast in November 2020 due to family illness, and returned to North Carolina where her family had settled during her teens 50 years ago. She now lives near Winston-Salem, but her heart remains in the Pacific Northwest.

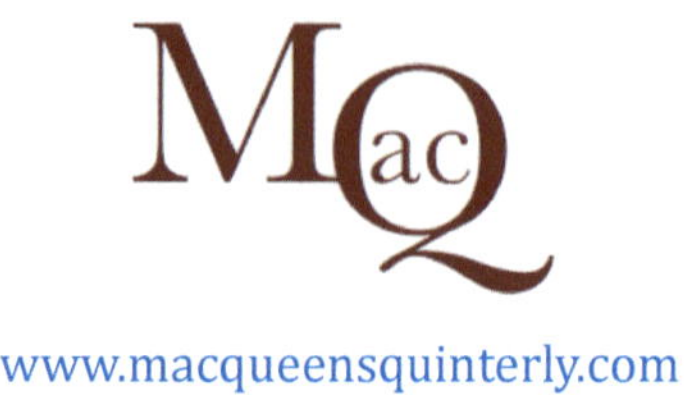